MONSTERS ARE REAL!

and other fun facts

To Birdie, my little monster!
—H. E.

To Maestra Banuelos: Thank you for your patience
and time in teaching my daughter.
—A. S.

LITTLE SIMON
An imprint of Simon & Schuster Children's Publishing Division
1230 Avenue of the Americas, New York, New York 10020
This Little Simon edition July 2016
Series concept by Laura Lyn DiSiena
Copyright © 2016 by Simon & Schuster, Inc.
All rights reserved, including the right of reproduction in whole or in part in any form.
LITTLE SIMON is a registered trademark of Simon & Schuster, Inc., and associated colophon is a trademark of Simon & Schuster, Inc.
For information about special discounts for bulk purchases, please contact Simon & Schuster Special Sales at 1-866-506-1949 or business@simonandschuster.com.
The Simon & Schuster Speakers Bureau can bring authors to your live event. For more information or to book an event, contact the Simon & Schuster Speakers Bureau at 1-866-248-3049
or visit our website at www.simonspeakers.com.
Manufactured in China 0516 SCP
10 9 8 7 6 5 4 3 2 1
This book has been cataloged with the Library of Congress.
ISBN 978-1-4814-6782-7 (hc)
ISBN 978-1-4814-6781-0 (pbk)
ISBN 978-1-4814-6783-4 (eBook)

DID YOU KNOW?

MONSTERS ARE REAL!

and other fun facts

By Hannah Eliot

Illustrated by Aaron Spurgeon

LITTLE SIMON

New York   London   Toronto   Sydney   New Delhi

Boo!

Did that scare you? No? Well, why don't you go look under your bed to make sure there aren't any monsters hiding there? You never know! Maybe that's where BIGFOOT lives!

Just kidding. Bigfoot would never fit under there! Did you know that Bigfoot is said to be between 7 and 8 feet tall, weighing between 300 and 800 pounds? And that he's covered in hair? How about that sightings have been reported all over the world for more than 400 years? It's true. In China, Australia, Indonesia, and all over the United States, there have been reports of Bigfoot. Did you know that there's a whole organization dedicated to researching the monster? It's called the Bigfoot Field Researchers Organization, and it's a community of scientists, journalists, and specialists.

No way. You knew all that? So do *you* believe in Bigfoot? Well, because there's no real physical evidence that Bigfoot exists, most scientists think the stories about the animal are folklore. But . . . did you know that *some* monsters ARE REAL?

So here's the deal. There are plenty of monsters that may or may not be real. And then there are also some *real* animals that were once thought to be monsters!

Take the PLATYPUS, for example. The first scientists to examine a platypus thought they were the victims of a hoax! Do you know what a hoax is? A hoax is meant to trick someone into believing something that isn't true. Did you know that platypuses spend most of their time hunting for food, and a hunt can last 10 to 12 hours? Or that platypuses are nocturnal, which means they are most active during the nighttime? Or that the platypus isn't a monster, after all?

How about the giraffe? That seems like a pretty cool yet pretty normal animal, right? The Chinese in the 1400s didn't think so. When a giraffe was gifted to Emperor Yongle, it was thought to be a *qilin*, otherwise known as a Chinese unicorn! But we know better now, and we can all agree that platypuses and giraffes are real animals!

One animal that is still rather mysterious is the GIANT SQUID. The largest giant squid ever found was 59 feet long and may have weighed close to 1 ton. So you'd think these guys would be pretty easy to spot in the water, right? Think again! Because the ocean is so vast and because giant squids live so deep underwater, they're rarely seen. This means that we really don't know much about them. How, you might wonder, did these animals evolve to *be* so big?

Well, some scientists think that the giant squid has very few predators, which means it can keep reproducing and continuing to grow. What scientists do know about the giant squid is that it has body parts just like other squids: 2 eyes, a beak, 8 arms, 2 feeding tentacles, and a funnel. A squid's funnel acts like a jet engine, drawing water in and then forcefully pushing it out to propel the squid! We also know that a giant squid's eyes are the size of dinner plates, making them the biggest eyes in the animal kingdom! Between the few things we do know and the mystery of all the things we *don't* know, this giant squid sure sounds like a monster, doesn't it?

The giant squid may also have something to do with a not-so-little monster called the KRAKEN. Even the name is scary, isn't it? The Kraken is a squid or octopus-like sea monster that is said to live off the coasts of Norway and Greenland.

Hey, did you know that nearly 80 percent of Greenland is covered by an ice cap and glaciers? Or that the World Ice Golf Championship usually takes place in Greenland every year? The course is cut into the ice between icebergs, and it continues out into the snowfields!

Norwegian tales of the Kraken from the 12th century often reference a creature so big that it is mistaken for an island or a *series* of islands! The Kraken is said to attack passing ships and create a whirlpool as it returns to the depths of the water. So if you plan to cross the seas around Greenland or Norway . . . WATCH OUT!

You may be more likely to come in contact with a *lake* monster than a *sea* monster. One of the most famous lake monsters is the LOCH NESS MONSTER, otherwise known by the friendlier name of "Nessie."

Do you know what a loch is? It's a lake or a bay or an arm of the sea that is nearly landlocked. And do you know where Nessie lives? In Loch Ness, of course! Loch Ness is in Scotland. The lake is nearly 800 feet deep and about 23 miles long, and holds more water than all of the lakes and rivers of England and Wales combined! Scotland is the United Kingdom's second-largest country, and it's home to one of the oldest trees in Europe! The twisted yew in Fortingall is estimated to be between 1,500 and 3,000 years old. Scotland also has the highest proportion of redheads in the world! About 13 percent of the population in Scotland has red hair.

But let's get back to Nessie. There are many theories about the monster. Some people think she's a living dinosaur, and some think she's a sea serpent that swam into the lake before it became landlocked.

Nessie is usually described as a creature with two humps, a long neck, a tail, and a little head. Sometimes the descriptions include flippers! Nessie first gained fame in 1933 when a story was published in a local newspaper about some splashing in the water. A year later, a photograph of Nessie was taken, though that was proven to be a hoax. Since then, tons of photos, films, and stories have surfaced, and we continue to search for Nessie. Divers and even mini submarines have looked for the monster. Some scientists have come up with different explanations for these sightings: eels in the loch, optical illusions, birds landing on the water and breaking the surface, and more. But other scientists think Nessie's still OUT THERE!

Nessie isn't the only lake monster we know of. Have you ever heard of OGOPOGO? This is the lake creature that supposedly lives in Okanagan Lake in British Columbia, Canada. Ogopogo is often described as having several humps on its back and a head that is said to look like that of a snake, seal, alligator, or even a horse or a sheep! Some people say Ogopogo has ears, and some say it has horns. Of *all* the lake monsters, Ogopogo is the best documented and the most likely to be real!

Then there's Champ, the lake monster who supposedly rules Lake Champlain, which is a lake in between New York and Vermont. The lake is named for the French explorer Samuel de Champlain, who is often said to have been the first one to spot the lake monster in 1609. He wrote in his journal of a sea serpent with large coils and scales.

There are other sea and lake monsters out there too!

The Brosno Dragon is said to live in Lake Brosno in Russia.

The Bunyip is a monster that supposedly lives in bodies of water ALL OVER Australia!

And Issie is a monster that some people believe lives in Japan's Lake Ikeda.

You're probably thinking that since most of these monsters live underwater, you're safe and sound on land. Unless you happen to be on a boat right now, or you are reading this book while swimming!

But what about VAMPIRES? Have you ever wondered about those guys? Vampires are said to have many different characteristics, but one thing we can all agree on is that they drink blood. CREEEEEPY! Some people say that vampires can turn into bats or wolves; that they don't cast a reflection in a mirror, water, or other reflective surfaces, and that sunlight scares them. Another way to scare off vampires is garlic. They can't stand the smell!

While the existence of vampires hasn't been proven, vampire BATS sure do exist. And do you know what makes them most like the vampires we were just talking about? These bats feed entirely on blood! Vampire bats sleep all day in complete darkness, usually hanging upside down in caves. They also live in the hollows of trees, as well as in abandoned buildings in Mexico and Central America and South America.

We've talked a lot about vampires, sea monsters, and giant ape-like creatures. And do you know that there's a name for all these creatures? They're called CRYPTIDS. A cryptid is an animal whose existence is disputed or unsubstantiated—meaning it hasn't been proven to be real. Here are a few different classifications of cryptids.

1) Unusual or oversize variations of known species (for example, GIANT anacondas reported in the Amazon)

2) Survivors of species believed to be EXTINCT (such as the ivory-billed woodpecker, thought to be extinct by 1960)

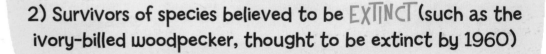

3) Survivors of species known only from the fossil record (for example, the Mokele-mbembe of Africa, which is believed to be a living DINOSAUR)

4) Hoaxes or misidentifications (like the JACKALOPE, which was a made-up rabbit with antlers!)

5) Mythical creatures that are based on REAL animals (The griffin—a half eagle, half lion—may have been inspired by a dinosaur called protoceratops!)

There's one mythological creature that has the same name and some of the same characteristics as a REAL animal. Do you know what it is? It's . . . the . . . DRAGON. Did you know that the word "dragon" comes from the ancient Greek word "*draconta*," which means "to watch"? This may suggest that the dragon is *watching over* its valuables, which is why we often see or read about dragons guarding treasure! Dragons are important to lots of different cultures, and they also mean very different things to those cultures. Dragons have appeared in Chinese history for more than 6,000 years. In China, dragons symbolize health, success, good luck, and power. The dragon is celebrated in parades and ceremonies. In Western cultures, however, the dragon may be seen as evil, greedy, and fire-breathing!

Now on to the REAL part. Have you ever heard of a Komodo dragon? Komodo dragons are the largest living lizards in the world! The average male Komodo dragon is 8 to 9 feet long and 200 pounds! The dragons can be different colors, including blue, orange, green, and gray. Komodos are extremely rare and can only be found in the wild on 5 Indonesian islands, where they've lived for MILLIONS of years!

Komodo dragons have an extremely good sense of smell and good vision, and they can run pretty fast too (up to 13 miles per hour)! All of this makes them excellent hunters.

The dragon has a forked tongue, and it actually uses the tongue to help smell. It sticks its tongue out to test the air. Then the dragon touches the tongue to the roof of its mouth, where it has special organs that analyze the molecules on the tongue. If the *left* tongue tip has more prey molecules, the dragon knows that its prey is to the left!

There are other mythical creatures that may have been based on real animals. Take the unicorn, the horse-like animal with a horn on top of its head.

Some people think the unicorn is based on an extinct animal called *Elasmotherium,* a huge rhinoceros that had a large single horn on its forehead and became extinct in the Ice Age. During the 1600s, tusks of narwhals were also thought to be unicorn horns! And then there's the oryx, an antelope with two straight horns on its head, that when viewed from the side looks like a unicorn, too!

There are lots of famous monsters that you've probably read about in books or seen in movies—characters such as Dracula, Godzilla, and King Kong.

Did you know that DRACULA may have been based on a real Romanian prince named Vlad III? Or that a castle in Romania called Bran Castle is thought to be where Dracula lived?

Did you know that the character GODZILLA was based on a combination of characteristics from *Tyrannosaurus rex*, an iguanodon, a stegosaurus, and an alligator? Or that his greatest weapon is "atomic breath" that he releases in the form of blue or red radioactive heat?

And then there's King Kong, the 50-foot-tall ape who climbed the Empire State Building! Did you know that King Kong's growl was created by playing a recording of a tiger roar *backward* and a lion roar *forward*?

Did you know that there was an *actual* giant ape called *Gigantopithecus*? It roamed the land about 300,000 years ago and was 10 feet tall and more than 1,000 pounds! Fossil remains of this creature may have inspired the stories of Bigfoot *and* the Yeti. What's that? You don't know what the Yeti is?

The Yeti is said to be an ape-like creature that roams the Himalayas of Nepal and Tibet. The Yeti is 6 feet tall and weighs about 300 pounds. You may also know the Yeti as the ABOMINABLE SNOWMAN. This name was coined in 1921 by a journalist who mistranslated the Tibetan label for the Yeti, "metoh-kangmi," which means "dirty men in the snow." But the search for the Yeti started well before 1921—way back in 326 BC, when Alexander the Great wanted to find the creature. Well, he didn't have much luck!

One of the Himalayan mountains the Yeti roams is Mount Everest. Did you know that Mount Everest is more than 29,000 feet tall, making it the highest peak on the ENTIRE PLANET? And did you know that the Himalayas continue to rise about 2 centimeters each year? How about that there are approximately 15,000 glaciers located throughout the Himalayan mountain range?

Some climbers claim to have seen an unusual animal on their way up Mount Everest. A few have even taken photographs of large footprints in the snow, claiming they belong to the Yeti.
Possible explanations for these sightings of the Yeti are that the creature was actually a black or brown bear—or even an *albino* black bear. And as for footprints that have been discovered, those too could have been made by real animals or they could have simply been the result of melting snow.

Speaking of the Yeti, have you ever heard of an animal called the YETI CRAB?

The Yeti crab was first observed in 2005 by marine biologists who discovered that this crab was an entirely new species! They named it the "Yeti crab" because of its hairy legs. Most of these crabs live more than 7,000 feet undersea, near areas where warm water seeps out of the seafloor, and often where lava has recently flowed!

And while there's no scientific evidence that proves the Yeti itself definitely exists, these Yeti crabs sure are REAL!

MORE FUN FACTS

Bigfoot: Russia, France, and Germany have all put Bigfoot on the endangered species list.

Yeti crab: Even though you just saw Yeti crabs with eyes, they actually *don't* have eyes! They may use their hairs as tiny sensors to help them find food in the deep sea.

Giraffe: Giraffes have four stomachs!

Cryptozoology: This is a pseudoscience, which means it's a science that doesn't follow valid scientific methods.

Lake monsters: Other lake monsters include the Lagarfljót worm in Iceland, Nahuelito in Argentina, and Inkanyamba in South Africa.

Dragon: In Greek and Roman times, it was thought that dragons understood the secrets of the earth.

Yeti: In 1960, Sir Edmund Hillary, the first man to scale Mount Everest, searched for evidence of the Yeti. He found what he thought was the scalp of the monster, but it turned out to be from a goat-like animal called a serow instead.

Komodo dragon: Komodo dragons are carnivores and will eat pretty much any part of another animal's body—including the bones!

Vampire bats: Vampire bats can walk, jump, and even run!

King Kong and Godzilla: There was a 1962 movie called *King Kong vs. Godzilla!*

Kraken: The image of the Kraken has been used in books, in movies, on TV, and even on postage stamps and a roller coaster!

Giant squid: The giant squid's huge eyes enable them to detect objects in the deep, dark waters of the ocean where they live.

Loch Ness monster: There have been more than 4,000 recorded sightings of Nessie!

Platypus: The platypus is one of only two mammals that lay eggs!